MW01092888

make
magic

also by Brad Meltzer

thrillers
The Lightning Rod
The Escape Artist
The House of Secrets
The President's Shadow
The Fifth Assassin
The Inner Circle
The Book of Lies
The Book of Fate
The Zero Game
The Millionaires
The First Counsel
Dead Even
The Tenth Justice

nonfiction
The JFK Conspiracy
The Nazi Conspiracy
The Lincoln Conspiracy
The First Conspiracy

children's books
The Ordinary People Change the World series
Heroes for My Daughter
Heroes for My Son

THE
BOOK OF
INSPIRATION
YOU DIDN'T
KNOW YOU
NEEDED

make
magic

Brad
Meltzer

wm
WILLIAM MORROW
An Imprint of HarperCollinsPublishers

For
Jonas, Lila, *and* Theo.
You know how much
I love being
your dad?

And in memory *of*
Greg Harden,
our secret weapon.

make
magic

introduction

What you hold in your hands is the commencement address I delivered when my son graduated from the University of Michigan in 2024.
To be clear, I also went to Michigan, so when I told my son Jonas that I would be the graduation speaker, his reaction was probably the same as many in the audience—and this is a direct quote of what my son said:

"YOU? Not Tom Brady? There's so many people they can pick. It's like a thirteenth seed winning March Madness!"

So first, thank you to the people who believe in the thirteenth seed. I'm counting you as one of them, dear reader. You're the reason this book exists.

To start at the beginning,

when I was giving this speech in Michigan Stadium, it was a stressful time. The graduates were born just before or in the aftermath of 9/11. Nineteen years later, COVID hit, taking millions of lives and turning their first years of college upside down. Indeed, *this* was their first proper graduation since middle school. We'd all been waiting so long for this day.

For me, though, in a stadium of seventy thousand people, I was focused on one: my son. To be honest, I was worried I wouldn't be able to find him in the crowd. But he and his friends arrived early, at 8:00 a.m., among the first hundred students to enter the stadium. From what I could gather, my son and his roommates had no idea if I was about to embarrass myself or become the next Winston Churchill. Yet, whatever the outcome, there they were, in the fourteenth row—my son in the aisle seat, staring straight at me.

It was
all that
mattered.

In these pages,

you'll read the content of the speech, but at its core, the messages within began with my three kids—and the magical shift from youth to adulthood. But really, it's packed with the very best lessons life has given me. As a parent, it took me a long time to realize that I've learned far more from my children than they've learned from me.

And yes, I had to edit some of the text, pulling out the parts that were specific to Michigan. We couldn't figure out a way to make Desmond Howard, J. J. McCarthy, and Blake Corum appear from nowhere—and if that reference doesn't make sense, google the original speech and watch it.

Trust me.

Here's the real point:

When you make your living speaking in front of people, you become hyper-attuned to audiences and their reactions. You never completely get it right, but it doesn't stop you from trying to predict when the crowd will laugh and when they'll applaud, so you can pause and let the performance breathe. On that day in Michigan Stadium, I thought I knew where all the high points would be— where the jokes would land and the laughter would come.

As usual, I was completely wrong. Indeed, as I delivered the words in these pages, what caught me completely off guard was the moment where I started talking about kindness and empathy.

Make no mistake,

it's my favorite part of the speech. I had high hopes—it's what I want most in the universe right now. At best, I thought it would get some claps and knowing nods. But on that day, a wave of energy nearly knocked me over as seventy thousand people interrupted me, refusing to let me speak, breaking into spontaneous applause. Because of kindness. Because of empathy.

It had nothing to do with me.
It's simply that, as a culture, we're exhausted by venom and cruelty—and we're starving for kindness and empathy, which is both inspiring and heartbreaking.

In the days and weeks that followed,
millions of strangers started
sharing those lessons online.
And now, I get to share them
once again with *you*, dear reader.
Thank you for believing in this message
and believing in the thirteenth seed.
You are proof that it's true:

"If you really want to shock the world, unleash your kindness."

Special thanks to

University of Michigan president Santa Ono and the regents—including Mark Bernstein, my Michigan classmate and dear friend— plus all the distinguished faculty, guests, and staff who gave me the opportunity of a lifetime by making this happen. My inner circle of Alisse Portnoy, Michele Norris, Steve Grafton, Larry Kirshbaum, and John Carson, plus Desmond Howard, Greg Harden, J. J. McCarthy, and Blake Corum, believed before anyone else.

Tremendous love to my wife and favorite magician, Cori, who I've adored since before freshman year; to my kids, Jonas, Lila, and Theo; and to so many friends who weighed in and helped hone early drafts: Wendy Shanker (who is a genius), Chris Weiss, Noah Kuttler, Jessica and Jason Herthel, Pansy Vore Price, Ethan Kline, Ali Arden, Matt and Jami Axelrod, Lisa

Stulberg and Evan Rudall, Matt Oshinsky, Joel Rose, David Lawrence, Jean Becker, Seth Reiss, and David Hacker, as well as Simon Sinek, Tim Urban, and Adam Grant, who helped brainstorm at the very start. Extra thanks to Jenny Freels, Michelle Vosters, Tami Wilkinson, Charles Rousseaux, Stephen Yaros, and Jay Mandel for managing every detail.

This book would not exist without Liate Stehlik, Emily Krump, Ben Steinberg, Kelly Rudolph, Mauro DiPreta, Ed Spade, Paige Meintzer, Jennifer Eck, David Palmer, Leah Carlson-Stanisic, Bonni Leon-Berman, and Stephanie Lindner; dear old friends Sharyn Rosenblum, Andy LeCount, and Ian Doherty; fearless leader Brian Murray, the best sales force in the business, and everyone else in my Harper/Morrow family—I so appreciate your faith.

Most of all, thank you to all the families, friends, and extraordinary students of the Class of 2024.

Get
ready
to
make
magic.

Finally, *and* certainly most importantly, Go Blue.

—Brad Meltzer,
Fort Lauderdale, Florida

We all have past versions of ourselves—every single one of us—including me.

At twenty-two years old,

I was graduating college.

It wasn't a great day for me.

My sister couldn't be there,

and without her as the buffer,

I was arguing even more

with my parents.

What I remember
most of all is that my college
held a competition to
be one of the student
speakers at graduation.
I wrote and submitted a
speech, thinking I'd win.

I didn't even make it
past the first round.

As I look at the journey—
twenty-two-year-old me back then,
·sitting in the audience, to fifty-four-year-
old me now, standing on this stage—it
defies all logic. There are many things
science and math can explain:

When someone offers
you a breath mint, take it.

Learn the
Uber driver's name.

If you're nice to me
and a jerk to the waiter,
you're a jerk.

But some things are unexplainable.

They're just *magic*.

As a writer,

that's my job—

making things

appear out of

thin air.

So that's what

I'd like to

discuss today:

How
to
make
magic.

Of course,

that sounds absurd—real magic doesn't exist. But when you ask professional magicians, they'll tell you there are actually only four types of magic tricks. That's it. Put aside illusions and escapes—there're just four types of tricks:

1. You make something appear.

2. You make something disappear.

3. You make two things switch places.

4. And finally, you change one thing into something else.

So.
The first
way for you
to make
magic:
You make
something
appear.

What you need to make appear is

YOU.

I'm not just talking about
showing up, but making the
best version of you appear.
We're all chameleons. We act
one way with our parents,
another way with our friends.

But as the writer Tim Urban explains, underneath all those Outer Yous is an Inner You that's who you really are deep down.

The ultimate version of you—the one where you feel the most confident and secure—where you're fully present and focused. That version only comes out with people you're comfortable with and who appreciate the *real* you—and love you for it.

When I graduated college, my
first job was in Boston, with a boss
who said he'd be my mentor.

I was so excited. But the week I
got to Boston, my boss left the job.
I thought my life was ruined.

So that night, in some run-down
sports bar, I told my girlfriend, "I
know what I'm gonna do with this
year"—what all of us would do in a
moment where we think our lives are
ruined: I said, *I'm gonna write a novel.*

My girlfriend
had the best
reaction of all.
She didn't
laugh—
she told me
to go write
the novel.

She believed
in that
version
of me.
That
girlfriend
gave me
lift.

When I finally wrote that book,

I got twenty-four rejection letters.

There were only *twenty*

publishers at the time,

and I got *twenty-four* rejection

letters. That means some

people were writing me twice

to make sure I got the point.

But I said, *If they don't like that book, I'll write another, and if they don't like that book I'll write another.* I realized I wanted to be a novelist. And my girlfriend? She didn't laugh at that, either. That next book *did* get published. I owe her forever for that lift she gave me.

Why do you think I married her? She helped me with this speech, helped me edit and refine. She's the mother of our kids. And can we take a moment and hear it for every strong mother, and father, and grandparent . . . whoever it is who helped raise you, whether they're with you today or not . . . let's hear it for those who got us to this day!

Something happened when I got that unconditional support from that girlfriend who became my wife. Professor Jane Dutton calls it a "reflected best-self portrait." When someone you trust sees your potential and says they believe you can be that person, it opens up a path and inspires you to become that version of yourself.

That's why
the friends
you graduate
with *matter.*
Hold tight
to them.

Their love and trust are key ingredients—because when you graduate, your mission is to make the best version of you appear. And then watch.

Surprise yourself.

Build something that can't be ignored.

We'll be the ones cheering.

Which leads to the second way to **make** *magic*: You make something *disappear*.

It's tempting to say that you should make fear disappear. But let me challenge that.

In high school, I had a job scooping ice cream at the Häagen-Dazs in the Aventura Mall. One day, this woman came up and snapped her fingers at me.

"You need to serve me!" she barked.

"Ma'am, I'll be right with you," I told her.

"Now!" she insisted.

We went back and forth, and eventually I said to her, "You're being rude, ma'am—I'm not serving you."

"You better serve me," she yelled.

And when I refused, she screamed in my face, "You're going to be working at this miserable ice cream store for the rest of your miserable life!"

And I calmly told her, "Ma'am, if I *am* working here for the rest of my miserable life, you're *still* never getting any ice cream."

For decades, I used to tell that story, laughing, saying, "It never even bothered me."

But I need to admit, it did bother me. It terrified me. My dad struggled financially his whole life, and it made me feel like *my* life would be filled with that same financial struggle. But I now also realize . . . that fear? That fear this woman brought out in me? It *fueled* me. It *drove* me.

Ever have

that feeling where

someone says,

"You can't do it"—

that you're done

and finished?

God, does it feel good to
fight back, to make them
eat those words and show
them they misjudged you.

So yes, make
your fear disappear

but not because fear is bad.

Use your fear.

Harness it.

Let them
underestimate you.

In the end,
don't vanquish
your critics,
prove them wrong.

Which leads me to the third way to make *magic*:

You make
two things
change places
with each other.
And here,
let's talk
about
empathy.

That's what

empathy is—

switching places

with someone else

and putting yourself

in their shoes.

When I was thirteen years old, my dad lost his job. He barely had any savings, and we had no place to live, so my parents moved us from Brooklyn, New York, to Miami, Florida, where my grandparents lived—so we could stay with them until we got back on our feet. For months, six of us—my mom, dad, sister, and myself, plus my two grandparents—lived in a tiny one-bedroom apartment.

Since it was Florida, all
the condo commandos
complained that we couldn't
have that many people in
such a small space. And then
one day, the neighbor across
the hall told my grandmother
that she'd leave her own
apartment—and give it to
my grandparents so we could
use it, so my family could
have some space and comfort
and not have to worry about
those who wanted to evict us.

I remember

her name as

Meercie,

which, as a kid, I always heard as

Mercy.

Make no mistake,

mercy—and empathy—

is what

she showed us.

Today, cruelty and venom—harshly judging those we disagree with—has become sport in our culture.

But cruelty and venom
aren't proof of strength;
they're signs of weakness . . .
and petty insecurity.

What takes strength
is switching places and
putting yourself in
someone else's shoes.

That's not easy.

In fact, studies show that when
we get too much bad news, our
brains get overwhelmed. That's
why we change the channel,
swipe to a new app, shut down.

Do not

shut down.

We need you.

If you shut down,

we're in

trouble.

Today, all around you, there are families experiencing divorce or financial hardship. Some of your fellow students are fighting cancer, a few are getting posthumous degrees since they passed away, many have buried parents and grandparents during their time at school.

Every family at your graduation has someone who they wish could be here today.

I wish my parents were

alive to see my kids today.

To see that we're okay.

As you go through life, every

person you encounter is battling

something you can't see.

The solution is

switching places

and

feeling empathy.

As the saying goes,

"One day, someone is

going to hug you so

tight that all of your

broken pieces will fit

back together."

The world
needs more
empathy,
more humility,
and, certainly,
more decency.
If you really
want to shock
the world,
*unleash your
kindness.*

That's a completely naïve idea. But it's an idea worth fighting for.

We talked about the magic of making something appear, making something disappear, and making two things switch places. Which leaves us with the final way to

make *magic*:

Changing one thing into something else.

The hardest trick of all.

Transformation.

Who you are today

isn't the person

you'll be in the future.

Graduation may feel

like a finale, but it's

not an end point.

So let me just say it:

Never
stop
changing.

When I was little,

my favorite thing at the
amusement park was the hall
of mirrors. Some people love
watching little kids crash into the
glass. I loved it because I had hair
back then—and it was *glorious.*

But what I really loved about
the hall of mirrors was how you
could turn your head just slightly,
and all those versions of you
would appear.
All the possibilities.

As we get older,

it's human nature to see just one
version—to get locked into ways
of thinking about the world, about
your life path, about who you are.
But as a friend recently told me,
when you write things in stone,
everything becomes hard and
brittle and starts collecting dust.

As you start

your next chapter,

write in pencil and

be unafraid to use

the eraser.

The person who
thinks they're
the smartest in
the room,
I promise you,
is not the smartest
in the room.
That's just the
one with the
most fragile ego.

The most sophisticated and intelligent people I know are the ones willing to challenge their thinking and admit there's more to learn.

Life will absolutely not
be what you think it will be.
It will be hard and wonderful
and messy and rewarding,
with more versions of you
than you think possible.

The only immutable

fact is,

you should

never be immutable.

Keep transforming,
learning, and never
think you know it all.
Instead, see yourself
in the hall of mirrors—

endless possibilities.

Now you
know the
four ways
to
make
magic:

You make the
best version of
YOU
appear, make
your fear
disappear and
harness it,
switch places to
find empathy,
and never stop
transforming.

So let me reveal the final step, what all *four tricks* have in common.

They take effort.

They take

you.

Things don't

just appear

or disappear

by themselves.

Making
magic,

figuring out who you are, takes

work,

time,

and

intentionality.

As the writer Simon Sinek
reminded me, that's how magic is:
full commitment to the bit,
or it all falls apart.

So many people sacrificed
to get you here.

But that love doesn't
dissipate.

Wherever you go, the
best part is, those people
never leave you.

You'll see.

What's coming up is the most
terrifying, impossible-to-predict
chapter of your life. And the most
exciting. Your first job. Your second
job. And your third. The silly hours.
The awful apartments. The broken
hearts. You'll wear clothes that you'll
swear will never go out of style
(hint: they'll go out of style) and
go on adventures that would haunt
you if you knew what was coming.

But what you'll remember more
than anything are those people who
cheered for you along the way.

No matter where you go,

or what beautiful mountains

you eventually climb,

when you see those people—

especially the friends you

made here—you'll instantly

be transported back to this

time . . . to this place . . .

like magic.

You'll make plans and do

your best to get together.

Sometimes you'll be too busy;

sometimes one of you will

have moved too far away.

Then, maybe one day, *you'll* be

the one sitting in the audience

to proudly watch your child,

like we're watching you—

the unstoppable student—

as they graduate.

And that's the best trick of all. You're graduating. You already won. That's it. You won.

Like I said, there are past versions of all of us.

And the only thing I know for sure is, if that past version of you could see you now, they would look at you . . . in awe.

As for the past version of
me, I see myself at twenty-
two, sitting in my own
cap and gown, thinking
about that rejected speech
I'd never get to give.

And it reminds me:

Magic is never for yourself.

It's a gift you give other people.

And that's the real reveal:
In our time together, I've used magic as metaphor, but real magic, the most powerful magic . . . *that* comes from making memories.

Memories that endure, like cherished friendships. Memories so powerful that even though they happened years ago, you can feel them now . . . see them now . . . conjured out of thin air.

That's the thing
about time
and memory—
they're slippery.

Which is

why the best

magicians always

have a final trick

up their sleeve.

Sometimes
magic
is hiding right
in front
of you the
entire time.

For a moment,
think about this book.

Not the lessons.
Not the stories.

Not even the

giant fonts

and fancy layout

designed to impress you.

Instead, focus solely on how this **book** got into your hands.

Think
of the
person
who
gave
it to
you

(even if you bought it for yourself).

Sure, this is
a book.
But it's
also a gift.

A compilation of
hopes and
possibilities for
future you.
A message in
a bottle sent now
to your future self.

This book
was put in
your hands because
someone
loves and
believes
in you.

And they know one
thing for sure . . .

Abrac

adabra

You

are

the

magician

now.

It's your
turn to take
the stage,
to reach into
your
magic hat,
and pull out
something
incredible.

Show 'em
what you got.

We can't
wait to see
what it is.

Don't ever forget:
The only people
who see

magic

are the
ones who
look for it.

make

magic.

Brad Meltzer is the Emmy-nominated, #1 *New York Times* bestselling author of *The Lightning Rod* and twelve other bestselling thrillers. He also writes nonfiction books like *The JFK Conspiracy* and the Ordinary People Change the World kids' book series.

Brad is also the host of *Brad Meltzer's Decoded* on the History Channel and is responsible for helping find the missing 9/11 flag with his show *Brad Meltzer's Lost History.*

Most important, when he gave the commencement address at the University of Michigan, even his kids liked it.

You found it.

Now make it appear.

The material on linked sites referenced in this book is
the author's own. HarperCollins disclaims all liability
that may result from the use of the material contained
at those sites. All such material is supplemental and
not part of the book. The author reserves the right
to operate or close the website in his sole discretion
following March 2025.

MAKE MAGIC. Copyright © 2025 by Forty-Four Steps,
Inc. All rights reserved. Printed in Canada. No part of
this book may be used or reproduced in any manner
whatsoever without written permission except in the
case of brief quotations embodied in critical articles
and reviews. For information, address HarperCollins
Publishers, 195 Broadway, New York, NY 10007.

HarperCollins books may be purchased for educational,
business, or sales promotional use. For information,
please email the Special Markets Department at
SPsales@harpercollins.com.

FIRST EDITION

DESIGNED BY BONNI LEON-BERMAN

Author photograph by Eric Bronson,
Michigan Photography, University of Michigan

Library of Congress Cataloging-in-Publication Data has
been applied for.

ISBN 978-0-06-344071-5

25 26 27 28 29 TC 10 9 8 7 6 5 4 3 2